GALATIANS

FREE
FOR ALL

8 INTERACTIVE BIBLE STUDIES FOR
SMALL GROUPS AND INDIVIDUALS

PHILLIP D. JENSEN
AND KEL RICHARDS

Free for All
Second edition
© Matthias Media 2010

First published 1994

Matthias Media
(St Matthias Press Ltd ACN 067 558 365)
PO Box 225
Kingsford NSW 2032
Australia
Telephone: (02) 9663 1478; international: +61-2-9663-1478
Facsimile: (02) 9663 3265; international: +61-2-9663-3265
Email: info@matthiasmedia.com.au
Internet: www.matthiasmedia.com.au

Matthias Media (USA)
Telephone: 724 964 8152; international: +1-724-964-8152
Facsimile: 724 964 8166; international: +1-724-964-8166
Email: sales@matthiasmedia.com
Internet: www.matthiasmedia.com

Scripture quotations are from The Holy Bible, English Standard Version, copyright © 2001 by Crossway Bibles, a publishing ministry of Good News Publishers. Used by permission. All rights reserved.

ISBN 978 1 921441 69 1

All rights reserved. Except as may be permitted by the Copyright Act, no part of this publication may be reproduced in any form or by any means without prior permission from the publisher.

Cover design and typesetting by Matthias Media.
Series concept design by Lankshear Design Pty Ltd.

» CONTENTS

How to make the most of these studies 5

STUDY 1: Damned angels and gospel twisters
[Galatians 1:1-10] 9

STUDY 2: Under attack
[Galatians 1:11-2:10] 17

STUDY 3: Faith + anything = nothing
[Galatians 2:11-21] 23

STUDY 4: From curse to blessing
[Galatians 3:1-18] 29

STUDY 5: Turning back the clock?
[Galatians 3:19-4:11] 37

STUDY 6: Christians: slaves or free?
[Galatians 4:12-5:12] 45

STUDY 7: Unnatural acts
[Galatians 5:13-26] 51

STUDY 8: Two ways to live
[Galatians 6] 57

GALATIANS

›› HOW TO MAKE THE MOST OF THESE STUDIES

1. What is an Interactive Bible Study?

Interactive Bible Studies are a bit like a guided tour of a famous city. They take you through a particular part of the Bible, helping you to know where to start, pointing out things along the way, suggesting avenues for further exploration, and making sure that you know how to get home. Like any good tour, the real purpose is to allow you to go exploring for yourself—to dive in, have a good look around, and discover for yourself the riches that God's word has in store.

In other words, these studies aim to provide stimulation and input and point you in the right direction, while leaving you to do plenty of the exploration and discovery yourself.

We hope that these studies will stimulate lots of 'interaction'—interaction with the Bible, with the things we've written, with your own current thoughts and attitudes, with other people as you discuss them, and with God as you talk to him about it all.

2. The format

Each study contains five main components:
- short sections of text that introduce, inform, summarize and challenge
- a set of numbered study questions that help you examine the passage and think through its meaning
- sidebars that provide extra bits of background or optional extra study ideas, especially regarding other relevant parts of the Bible
- an 'Implications' section that helps you think about what these passages mean for you and your life today
- suggestions for thanksgiving and prayer as you close.

3. How to use these studies on your own

- Before you begin, pray that God would open your eyes to what he is saying in the Bible, and give you the spiritual strength to do something about it.
- Work through the study, reading the text, answering the questions about the Bible passage, and exploring the sidebars as you have time.
- Resist the temptation to skip over the 'Implications' and 'Give thanks and pray' sections at the end. It is important that we not only hear and understand God's word, but respond to it. These closing sections help us do that.
- Take what opportunities you can to talk to others about what you've learnt.

4. How to use these studies in a small group

- Much of the above applies to group study as well. The studies are suitable for structured Bible study or cell groups, as well as for more informal pairs and triplets. Get together with a friend or friends and work through them at your own pace; use them as the basis for regular Bible study with your spouse. You don't need the formal structure of a 'group' to gain maximum benefit.

- For small groups, it is *very useful* if group members can work through the study themselves *before* the group meets. The group discussion can take place comfortably in an hour (depending on how sidetracked you get!) if all the members have done some work in advance.
- The role of the group leader is to direct the course of the discussion and to try to draw the threads together at the end. This will mean a little extra preparation—underlining the sections of text to emphasize and read out loud, working out which questions are worth concentrating on, and being sure of the main thrust of the study. Leaders will also probably want to work out approximately how long they'd like to spend on each part.
- If your group members usually don't work through the study in advance, it's extra important that the leader prepares which parts to concentrate on, and which parts to glide past more quickly. In particular, the leader will need to select which of the 'Implications' to focus on.
- We haven't included an 'answer guide' to the questions in the studies. This is a deliberate move. We want to give you a guided tour of the Bible, not a lecture. There is more than enough in the text we have written and the questions we have asked to point you in what we think is the right direction. The rest is up to you.

5. Bible translation

Previous editions of this Interactive Bible Study have assumed that most readers would be using the New International Version of the Bible. However, since the release of the English Standard Version in 2001, many have switched to the ESV for study purposes. So with this new edition of *Free for All*, we have decided to quote from and refer to the ESV text, which we recommend.

STUDY 1

DAMNED ANGELS AND GOSPEL TWISTERS

[GALATIANS 1:1-10]

1. People often think that we can never be certain about the answers to religious questions such as "Who is God?" Why is this, do you think?

2. What answers do people give to the question, "What is a Christian?"

3. How would you answer that question?

What is a Christian?

IS THE ANSWER JUST A MATTER OF opinion? Our world today thinks that this question—and many others like it—is just a matter of opinion.

The world today is more lost than ever on the subject of what can and can't be known. There is a great lack of confidence about what is certain, as more and more things fall into the category of 'relative'.

Today no-one is right—except the person who says "no-one is right": he is always right!

Every point of view is tolerated today, except the view that says there is right and wrong, true and false.

But in Galatians we will discover that God says that following Jesus Christ is not just a matter of opinion. There is a right, there is a wrong—there is true, there is false—about Christianity.

Read Galatians 1:8-9.

4. What tone does Paul adopt when discussing the preachers of a "gospel contrary to the one we preached"?

5. Why can't there be more than one gospel? Why is it such a serious issue?

6. What clues do you find here to the problems in the Galatian church?

The problem of confusion

PAUL HAD PREACHED THE gospel in **Galatia**, and founded churches there. He is writing to these churches because something has happened—troublers have come among them: "there are some who trouble you and want to distort the gospel of Christ" (v. 7).

Who were these troublers? They were people who were confusing what it means to be a Christian.

As we shall see later in Galatians, they were attacking Paul and the gospel by insisting on obedience to the Jewish law, as symbolized in **circumcision**.

But these Galatians were Gentiles (non-Jews) and they were uncircumcised—they had never taken the law upon themselves. Can these non-Jews become Christians without becoming Jews first? That is the question the 'troublers' were using to confuse the Galatians.

At first glance, this question has nothing much to do with us. But in these studies we shall find the same type of mistake being made today that the 'troublers' made back in the first century.

Paul's unusual greeting

Every culture has standard forms of greetings to use in letters. For example, today we might write:

> Dear Aunt Agatha,
>
> Thank you for the Christmas present—an elephant's foot umbrella stand is just what I have always wanted.
>
> Yours sincerely,
> Frank

The first century had a standard form for letters that went like this:

i. The writer's name
ii. The people to whom he was writing
iii. Greetings!

You can see this standard form throughout the New Testament. However, the Christian form was slightly differ-

Galatia
Galatia is Turkey, roughly speaking. The exact geographical boundaries wobble around a bit, but what Paul called Galatia is, more or less, part of modern Turkey.

Circumcision
For the Jew in the Old Testament (from Genesis 17 onwards), circumcision (the surgical removal of the foreskin of the penis) was the sign of being 'under contract' with God, the contract that gave rise to the law. It was the symbol of accepting the Old Testament law as the system that ruled your life. This is stated in Galatians 5:3: "I testify again to every man who accepts circumcision that he is obligated to keep the whole law".

ent—instead of "Greetings!", Christians would write "Grace to you and peace!"

Paul also had his own standard letter form. It generally went like this:

i. Paul, an apostle of Jesus Christ
ii. To the church in ...
iii. Grace and peace to you
iv. I always thank God for you because of ...
v. And I am praying for you ...

Read Galatians 1:1-10.

7. In what ways does Paul's greeting differ from his standard greeting (above)?

8. What does Paul say about what it means for him to be an apostle (v. 1)?

9. What does Paul say about the source of grace and peace?

10. Paul is astonished that the Galatians are deserting the gospel of Christ (v. 6). What do we learn about the gospel of Christ in this passage (vv. 1-10)?

What is the gospel?

The giving

THE KEY WORD HERE IS GRACE (vv. 3, 6), and it means 'generosity'. It is the opposite to something we have earned, something we do for ourselves.

If at the end of a week's work your boss gives you a week's pay, that is not generosity; it is just what you have earned—what you deserve or merit because of what you have done. But if you don't turn up for work and the boss still hands you a packet of money—that is grace. That is surprising (astonishing!) generosity, and is entirely unearned.

Grace and merit are opposites. You cannot get something both by grace and by merit at the same time. It is either one or the other. You either earn something or you are given it.

And grace—astonishing generosity—is what we get from Jesus. Paul wants to drive home that Jesus "gave himself for our sins to deliver us from the present evil age" (v. 4).

The Galatians are turning away from God who has called them through this astonishing generosity—this self-giving—of Jesus Christ (vv. 6-7).

The deserting

"I am astonished", writes Paul in verse 6, "that you are so quickly deserting him who called you in the grace of Christ and are turning to a different gospel".

Verses 7, 8 and 9 then tell us some amazing things about the character of the gospel that makes the idea that 'all religious truth is just a matter of opinion' absolute nonsense.

In these verses, the point is that there is only one true gospel—the gospel of the grace of Jesus Christ. But, there are also 'gospel twisters'—people who try to pervert (or twist) the gospel of grace.

And Paul makes another point: the authority of the gospel rests in the gospel message itself—not in the preacher of the gospel, however impressive that preacher might be. Don't even trust an angelic preacher, says Paul, only trust the one true gospel of grace.

So, if an angel (or an apostle!) tries to sell you a different gospel, says Paul, don't buy it!

Re-read Galatians 1:1-10.

11. What reasons does Paul give for being so insistent on the gospel of grace?

12. Which words (that Paul uses) convey the importance that Paul attaches to the gospel of grace?

13. When this letter was read for the first time, what did verses 1-10 tell the Galatian Christians about themselves?

Drawing the line

THERE IS ONLY ONE GOSPEL—THE gospel of the grace, the self-giving, of Jesus. There is no other gospel. It is either this or nothing.

"That's intolerant!" comes the protest.

Yes! God is intolerant about untruth.

Is it tolerant to say that the earth is both flat and round? There are some issues where 'tolerance' amounts to foolishness, and the truth of the gospel is one of them.

If Jesus Christ is God—then Krishna isn't. And Allah isn't.

That's exactly the same as saying that if the world is round, then it isn't flat.

In Galatians, God is telling us that there is no other gospel. There is no other way back home. It is this or nothing.

» Implications

(Choose one or more of the following to think about further or to discuss in your group.)

- How would you answer the person who says, "Religion is just a matter of opinion—people should believe whatever is true for them"?

- How does Paul's 'drawing the line' (vv. 8-9) affect the way we share the gospel with our friends from other religious backgrounds?

- What guidelines does Galatians 1:1-10 give us for exposing counterfeits of Christianity? What characteristics does it give us of the true gospel?

- How faithful have you been to the one true gospel? (In your conversations with non-Christians, have you been tempted to make it more palatable? Have you been tempted to trim the gospel to make it more attractive to your listeners? What experiences have you had with people who have tried to pervert the gospel?)

» Give thanks and pray

- Give thanks for God's word in Galatians and ask that he would change you through it.
- Give thanks that he has given us the one true gospel—the gospel of Jesus Christ.
- Ask God to help you proclaim this gospel in your life.

» STUDY 2
UNDER ATTACK
[GALATIANS 1:11–2:10]

1. What kinds of attacks on Christianity do you hear today?

2. Have you ever been attacked for being a Christian? If so, how did you handle it?

3. Was it you or was it the gospel under attack? How did this show itself?

Paul under attack

ATTACKS ON THE GOSPEL MESSAGE—and its messengers—often have the benefit of clarifying the issues involved in the gospel. For example, Paul was attacked for not being a proper apostle, and for not being a proper Jew. These attacks drove Paul to explain the source of his gospel message and of his commission to spread that message. They also pushed Paul to explain the relationship between being Christian and being Jewish.

Read Galatians 1:11-2:10.

4. Where did Paul get his gospel from (1:12)?

5. Before his conversion, which Christian preachers explained the gospel to Paul?

6. What evidence does Paul give to prove his Jewishness?

7. What was unusual about Paul's conversion? (Compare 1:16 with Acts 26:12-18.)

8. Why did Paul go to Jerusalem the first time (1:18)? Who did he meet?

9. Why did he go to Jerusalem the second time (2:2)? Who did he meet with this time (2:6-9)?

Paul's response

PAUL DID NOT INSIST THAT GENTILES be circumcised, nor did he insist that they follow the Jewish rules about eating—rules that spelled out who you could eat with, when, where and how.

All this upset 'the troublers' who (apparently) claimed that what Paul did was different to what the 'big name' apostles in Jerusalem did.

Paul's response was twofold.

1. He said that he was not under the authority of the 'big name' apostles in Jerusalem. The gospel, said Paul, had come to him directly by revelation from God, and, hence, he was under God's authority, not the authority of other apostles.
2. He said that what he preached was in full fellowship with the Jerusalem authorities. Although Paul was independent of the Jerusalem authorities, his message was the same as theirs: it was the true gospel.

Paul makes the point that before his conversion he did not hear the gospel from any Christian preacher. Indeed, before his conversion Paul's only contact with Christians was to persecute them (1:13-14)! In fact, Paul did not hear the gospel from any human being (1:12). Then, says Paul, God himself revealed the gospel to me (1:15-16), and he did so "in order that I might preach him [Jesus] among the Gentiles" (1:16).

Immediately after his conversion Paul went off to preach the gospel in Arabia—without bothering to check whether he had any human permission to do so (1:17). Paul did (eventually) go to Jerusalem to talk to the big wigs—the first time three years after his conversion (1:18), and again 14 years later (2:1).

He went because God told him to go. Paul's concern was that he might run his race in vain (2:2). This may mean that he was worried that those who thought Christians needed to be Jewish would ruin his work. It seems likely that, by coming to Jerusalem to present his gospel message, Paul was actually checking out the authenticity of the Jerusalem Christians, rather than the other way around!

Read Galatians 2:6-10.

10. What did Paul set out to explain at his meeting with James, Peter and John (2:2)?

11. What conclusion did James, Peter and John come to about the place in God's work given to Paul?

12. What did they base this on?

13. In looking at the mission field, how did the apostles see God at work in Paul and in Peter (and the others)?

God's gospel

DURING PAUL'S VISIT TO JERUSALEM he had with him an uncircumcised Christian—Titus. Paul resisted attempts to compel Titus to be circumcised. Why? "So that the truth of the gospel might be preserved for you" (2:5).

This was Paul drawing the line.

The **circumcision of Titus**, he said, was a matter of the gospel itself—it was fundamental, not a 'side issue'.

The point is that there is a world of difference between being compelled to be circumcised (or baptized, or taking part in any religious ceremony) as a legalistic requirement to be saved—and choosing freely to be circumcised (or baptized, or whatever) to facilitate ministry.

The issue of circumcision highlights the greatness of the gospel. Law-keeping is not the way to God. The way to God is through God's way to us—namely Jesus, who died for our forgiveness. The way to God is not by being 'good', but being forgiven!

That is God's gospel, which is the only gospel there is.

Paul knew that it was worth being attacked over this issue. He stood firmly for the gospel, in order that the truth would remain in the worldwide church. We need to follow Paul's example. If drawing the line means being attacked for what we believe, even by those who (falsely) claim to be our brothers and sisters (2:4), so be it. We must never jeopardize the truth of the gospel of free grace.

Was Titus circumcised?

The truth is that we don't know! All we know is that he wasn't compelled to be circumcised. He might, like Timothy (Acts 16:3) have chosen to be circumcised if that would assist his gospel ministry. But it is more than likely that he was not.

» Implications

(Choose one or more of the following to think about further or to discuss in your group.)

- If you were criticized for not believing in the authentic gospel of God's free grace, how would you defend yourself?

- How can we make sure that the true gospel is being preached in our churches?

- Is there any part of church life that should be considered essential to salvation? Do any of your church's rituals or customs actually jeopardize the gospel of God's free grace?

- The Rev. Matt Johnson is minister at St Basil's-by-the-Abattoir. A woman in the congregation approaches Matt with a problem: she has been a Christian for seven years but for one reason or another has never been baptized, either as an adult or an infant. Someone from another church has now told her that she cannot be saved without being baptized. What should Matt say or do? Give your reasons.

- Is the true gospel of God's free grace at stake in his decision? Give your reasons.

» Give thanks and pray

- Thank God that the gospel of Jesus Christ proceeds from him alone.
- Pray that we would preach only the gospel of true grace, and that we would protect it wisely from those who would try to add to it.

» STUDY 3

FAITH + ANYTHING = NOTHING

[GALATIANS 2:11-21]

1. Surveys show that the vast majority of people still believe in God. In your view, how do most people think they can get right with God and be accepted by him?

The war with the law

THE BIG CHALLENGE TO THE gospel in Paul's day and in our day is the same—it is law-keeping—and Galatians is about the struggle between the true gospel of the free grace of God and law-keeping.

Study 1 showed us the gospel of grace, and Paul's concern that the Galatian Christians were deserting it. Study 2 examined Paul's claim to preach the true gospel, and how he was attacked over his refusal to bow to pressure to circumcise Titus.

In this next section of Galatians, we

will see Paul further explaining the enormous difference between law-keeping and the gospel. The difference is apparent in a number of ways, but this letter deals with it chiefly in relation to circumcision (2:3) and food rules (2:12).

Prior to the writing of Galatians, the two apostles—Peter and Paul—had clashed in Antioch (2:11), where the first Gentile church had met. The cause of the conflict was the relationship between Jewish and Gentile Christians and, in particular, Peter's decision to stop eating with the Gentile Christians. To understand something of Peter's background to this clash, we need to turn to Acts 10.

Read Acts 10.

2. Why did Peter have doubts about eating certain foods?

3. Before the vision, why would Peter have been reluctant to visit Cornelius' house (v. 28)?

4. What was so surprising to the Jewish (the 'circumcised') Christians (v. 45)?

5. Why did Peter baptize Cornelius and his family (v. 47; Acts 11:17)?

By the time of Paul's letter to the Galatians, there were Christian Jews and non-Jews, who had once been poles apart, calling each other 'brother' and 'sister'.

But what sort of members of the Christian church could non-Jews be? Full members? Or only associate members? And if they were to be full members, did this mean they had to take on the whole of Judaism as well? Like not eating certain foods? Like being circumcised?

In the last study we looked at the significance of circumcision for the truth of the gospel. In Galatians 2:11-21, the focus is on eating. But once again, in this historical circumstance, the issue that is really being wrestled with is law-keeping versus the good news of God's free gift in Jesus Christ.

Read Galatians 2:11-21.

6. Why did Peter stop eating with the non-Jewish Christians in Antioch?

7. Why did Paul confront Peter over this issue?

8. Paul is writing to the Galatians, telling them of his confrontation with Peter in Antioch, because it has direct bearing on their own struggles with law-keeping. Just as Peter's actions weren't "in step with the truth of the gospel", so Paul is beginning to build his argument that those who are troubling the Galatians are also not acting in line with the gospel. In verses 15-21, he proceeds to spell out what it is about the gospel that made Peter's treatment of the Gentile brothers so inappropriate. What do these verses say about:

- how we are *not* justified before God (that is, declared right with him)?

- how we *can* be justified?

- the relationship of the Christian to the law?

- the consequences of going back to law-keeping?

9. How does all this show Peter's actions to be wrong?

10. Fill in the following table from verses 15-21:

	At the start of the Christian life	Throughout the Christian life
The place of the law		
The place of faith in Christ		

Today's challenge

THE TEMPTATION TO WITHDRAW from table fellowship with Gentile Christians because of Jewish food laws is not one that most Christians today have to deal with. To start with, most of us are Gentiles.

However, the temptation is always for us to see some form of law-keeping as the way to get right with God, or to stay right with God.

In terms of getting right with God, it is frighteningly common to hear people speak of the Ten Commandments or the Sermon on the Mount or some other ethical standard as being the way to get right with God. If we make a reasonable fist of keeping these and being good, they say, then God is bound to accept us in the end.

However, this sort of thinking betrays a low view of God and the law, and a high view of ourselves. We need to realize that the God we are seeking to please is a consuming fire, an awe-inspiring God of blindingly pure holiness who cannot tolerate any sin. He is no easy God to please. What is worse, despite our best intentions, we are all woeful at law-keeping. When we actually compare our behaviour with the Ten Commandments or the Sermon on the Mount, we come up embarrassingly short.

For Christians—that is, for those of us who have realized how far short we fall and have cast ourselves on Jesus Christ—there is still a danger in law-keeping. Having abandoned the law as a means of being right before God, there is no going back. It is not as if, having been declared right with God through Jesus' death alone, we then take up a regime of observing the law in order to remain Christians. In Paul's words, we cannot rebuild what we have destroyed. By trusting in Christ for our righteousness, we have utterly abandoned the path of law-keeping. We have died to it, says Paul. That part of us has been crucified with Christ, and our new life with Christ is lived out in trusting him (i.e. faith).

This was Peter's mistake. By drawing back from full fellowship with his Gentile brothers, he was going back to the law. He was trying to resurrect what was dead and buried; he was trying to rebuild what he had destroyed when he trusted in Christ. To attempt to add law-keeping to faith was to destroy what faith was all about.

» Implications

(Choose one or more of the following to think about further or to discuss in your group.)

- In what ways can we as Christians be tempted to get right with God through rules and law-keeping or good works?

- Is the motivation different for keeping God's laws for Christians and non-Christians?

- How does Christ's death demonstrate the inadequacy of law-keeping as a way to heaven?

- Many, perhaps most, non-Christians think that law-keeping (or some vague attempt at it) is the way to get right with God. Write down a short, point-by-point plan for explaining the gospel of God's free grace to a friend who thinks this way.

» Give thanks and pray

- Give thanks that we have been crucified with Christ, and so Christ lives in us.
- Pray that you would not be tempted to see law-keeping as a way to get right with God.

» STUDY 4
FROM CURSE TO BLESSING
[GALATIANS 3:1-18]

1. How do most people think about Jesus (when they stop to give him any serious thought at all)? What are they likely to say about Jesus?

The cursed Jesus

Jesus was a common criminal, a blasphemer, a phoney and a failure.

At least, that is what Paul thought when his name was still Saul and he was busy persecuting Christians. Saul/Paul believed that Jesus had obviously been cursed by God. The evidence was that he had been executed—crucified. Saul/Paul knew that the Bible said that "Cursed is everyone who is hanged on a tree" (3:13, quoting Deuteronomy 21:23).

To Saul/Paul, Jesus was a disaster

area! To call him the Christ, the Messiah, was perverse and peculiar. This assessment underwent a radical transformation when he went to Damascus to persecute Christians living there. Because on the road he met the 'cursed' Jesus, risen from the dead. And his whole way of thinking about life was radically transformed by that revelation.

The persecutor became the proclaimer, and went about preaching the gospel that he had tried to exterminate. It was this redeemed and reformed Paul who stood up in front of the Galatians and by his words clearly portrayed Jesus Christ as crucified (3:1b).

A three-stage argument

Under the preaching of the transformed Paul many people were themselves transformed, including the people in Galatia to whom Paul is writing this letter.

But after Paul moved on, and the 'law-keepers' we learned about in study 3 came on the scene, the Galatians lost the plot. Paul reminds them here that it was by believing the gospel of God's free grace through Jesus Christ—not observing the law—that they received the Holy Spirit. He supports this statement with a three-pronged argument and an example.

Read Galatians 3:1-14.

Stage 1: The argument from experience (vv. 1-5)
Paul first reminds the Galatians of their past reality, of what happened when they first received the gospel.

2. What answer is Paul expecting to the question he asks in verse 2?

3. According to verse 2, at what point in a Christian's life is he/she filled with the Holy Spirit? Is it:
   - when he/she believes the gospel of the crucified and risen Jesus?
   - when he/she is perfectly obedient to God?
   - when other Christians lay hands on him/her?
   - some other point in the Christian life?
   - impossible to say?

4. What are the Galatians now trying to add to belief in the gospel message they heard?

5. What does that make them in Paul's eyes?

6. Why have these Galatians needed to call on the courage and endurance that the Spirit gives?

7. What evidence of the work of the Spirit have these Galatians seen with their own eyes?

Stage 2: The argument from Abraham (vv. 6-9)
As he does in Romans, Paul then turns to Abraham, the Father of the Jews, as an ally in his argument against 'law' as a way to be righteous.

8. Abraham's righteousness: on what basis did Abraham receive the miraculous gift of righteousness (v. 6)? (Also check out the passage Paul is quoting here: Genesis 15:6.)

9. Abraham's children: What defining characteristic identifies a person as a true descendant of Abraham?

10. Abraham's blessing: The Scriptures knew that blessing would flow through Abraham, but who receives this blessing (vv. 8-9)? (Also check out the passages being referred to here: Genesis 12:3, 18:18 and 22:18.)

11. How does Abraham's blessing—the miraculous gift of righteousness—come?

Stage 3: The argument from Christ (vv. 10-14)

12. What is the immediate contrast between verses 10 and 11?

   Through _____ we receive _____ .

   Through _____ we receive _____ .

13. Why is this?

14. How much of the law do you have to keep to avoid the curse of the law?

15. Why is no-one justified by the law?

16. How are faith and law opposed?

17. How does Jesus redeem us?

18. Why did Jesus redeem us?

19. How does verse 14 summarize the whole argument (from vv. 1-13)?

JESUS BUYS US OUT OF THE CURSE OF the law—by becoming cursed himself, in our place. He redeems us—pays a ransom for us. How? By being "hanged on a tree", says Paul—arguing from Scripture. Paul has come full circle, back to the same idea that obsessed him when he was Saul, persecutor of Christians. But now he understands that Jesus suffered that curse *on our behalf!*

Being in the Spirit

It is worth pausing to consider what this passage teaches us about receiving the Spirit.

First, notice the centrality of the cross of Jesus. You can't get around the cross. The only way to receive the Spirit is by faith in the cross of Christ. It is through Jesus suffering our curse and being executed that we are redeemed and filled with the Holy Spirit. This is how we start with the Spirit and this is how we finish—it is all through Christ crucified.

Second, notice that receiving the Spirit is part of God's historic plan. There are not two gospels, nor two plans of God. God didn't start down one track in the Old Testament and then revert to plan B in the New Testament. His plan to pour out his Spirit on his people went all the way back to his promises to Abraham. Notice how the passage describes God's promise to Abraham as 'the gospel' announced in advance (v. 8).

Third, notice that the Spirit is for all the nations. In fulfilment of the promise to Abraham, God has included all people—Jews and Gentiles—in his plan. The Spirit comes to all who abandon human effort and put their trust in Jesus Christ crucified.

An example: giving by promise

To make his point clear, Paul now illustrates his three-fold argument with an example from how a human contract works.

Read Galatians 3:15-18.

20. What was the basis of God's dealings with Abraham?

21. To whom were the promises spoken (v. 16)?

To _____ (a)

and to _____ (b)

22. Who is (b) (v. 16)?

22. Can God's covenant contract—his promise—be nullified by the law?

23. What does our inheritance depend on?

» Implications

(Choose one or more of the following to think about further or to discuss in your group.)

- What would cause Paul to write to you, "Oh foolish Christian!"? What is likely to cause you to lose the plot and take your eyes off the gospel?

- What kinds of rules and regulations are today's Christians tempted to view as a way to God?

- List some rules that people have told you that you should follow in order to be a 'real' Christian, or a 'serious' Christian.

- Discuss some of the rules above in light of what you've learned from the study.

» Give thanks and pray

- Give thanks that God has justified the Gentiles by faith, and that he has kept his promise to bless all the nations through Abraham.
- Pray that our lives would change to more clearly reflect the free grace of God given to us.
- Ask God to protect you from the temptation of elevating rules and regulations above his grace.

STUDY 5

TURNING BACK THE CLOCK?

[GALATIANS 3:19-4:11]

1. When you become an adult, how does your attitude change towards the rules you had to keep as a child?

The purpose of the law

So far in Galatians, we have been onlookers to a battle between 'law' and 'faith'. Paul has been vigorously defending the gospel of grace from attack by those who would require Gentile Christians to fully obey the Old Testament law.

No-one is justified by law-keeping, Paul has thundered. There is only one way to be declared right with God, and that is through Christ's death on the cross. It is the only way, and if you try to add law-keeping to faith as an additional requirement, you have misunderstood the whole thing and destroyed the very essence of faith. The blessings promised to Abraham flow out to the Gentiles through faith, not through the law. If you want to be a true Jew, a true child of Abraham, then receive the promise by faith, just as Abraham did. This has been Paul's argument up to this point.

All this leaves one big question hanging: What purpose *does* the Old Testament law serve? If the Spirit was not poured out through law-keeping, but through the gospel of grace, then why did God bring in the law in the first place? What place does the law have for the Christian life?

It is to this question that Paul now turns in his letter.

Read Galatians 3:19-4:7.

2. What does Paul say is the purpose of the law (3:19, 24)?

3. The law was "added" until ... when? Note down the different ways this 'when' is described.

4. Who is the "offspring" (3:19)?

5. In 3:25-29, Paul switches from talking about "we" to talking about "you".
   - Who do you think are the "we"?

   - Who are the "you"?

6. Now that the law is no longer operational (as a guardian or jail-keeper), what does this do to the barriers between Jews and Gentiles?

7. Who can now be one of Abraham's "offspring", and how?

Sons not slaves

IN THE SECTION WE'VE BEEN READING, Paul uses several images to describe the place and purpose of the Old Testament law. He describes it as a jail-keeper who kept God's people locked up or restrained until Christ came. He describes it as a school teacher or childminder (this is what the Greek word in 3:24 means; the ESV renders it **"guardian"**). He describes it as a manager. These are images that Paul's readers would have well understood.

All these images emphasize that the law God gave to Old Testament Israel was a temporary measure. Its role was to restrain and educate; to put a brake on sinfulness and set boundaries inside which God's people could live until Christ came. Its function was never to save or justify, says Paul. Now that faith in Christ has come, the law is no longer in charge. It is no longer a supervisor. We are no longer slaves, but sons and heirs.

In all of this, we must remember that the people who were troubling the Galatian church were from a Jewish background. They were trying to persuade the Galatians that, whether they were Jewish or not, they needed to keep the whole Old Testament law if they were going to be genuine Christians.

In reply to these troublers, Paul is saying that the Old Testament law was a temporary measure in God's plan. It applied to the Old Testament people of God (the Israelites) until Christ came, but now its supervisory role is over. It is no longer the supervisor—not of Jews any more, and certainly not of Gentiles—because now Christ has come. Now all can inherit the promise to Abraham; now all can be sons of God through trusting in Jesus Christ.

Let's read on.

Guardians in the Old Testament

In the ancient world, it was common for a well-educated slave to be put in charge of the 'son' and 'heir' of a wealthy family. This slave would train, teach, discipline and exercise complete control over the child. When childhood and youth were past and the young man was of age, he would come into his inheritance. Then their positions would be reversed. The slave would now be under the command of the heir.

Read Galatians 4:1-11.

8. In what sense were the Jews (the "we" of verse 3) under slavery to "elementary principles"?

9. What was the time limit to their slavery?

10. How did God free them from their slavery?

11. On what basis can people become sons of God? Is this the same for everyone?

12. What are the privileges of being one of God's sons?

13. In what sense were Paul's Gentile readers (the "you" in verse 8) also at one time under slavery to **"principles"**?

14. What would going back to law-keeping and religious observances mean for these Gentiles?

No turning back

CAN YOU IMAGINE NELSON MANDELA, freed from imprisonment after 25 years and then President of South Africa, going back to jail and asking to be locked up again? Can you imagine a student finally graduating from university after years of education, re-enrolling in primary school? Can you imagine a street kid picked up from the gutter and adopted into a warm, accepting family, choosing to go back to homelessness?

This is the level of astonishment Paul shows towards the Galatians. He can't believe that they are doing what they are doing. Why go back to slavery? God freed you from all the pagan mumbo-jumbo and religious observances of your old life, and adopted you into his very own family through faith in his Son. Why on earth would you want to go back to law-keeping?

Again and again in this letter to the Galatians, we have been taught these sorts of things. The gospel of God's grace in Christ has freed us from the slavery of the law. It has freed us from being 'religious' and trying to please God through doing certain things— whether they are the things of God's own Old Testament law, or the things of human religion.

First principles

These are tricky verses, easier to understand if you realize that Paul is using a play on words that doesn't come out well in the English. The Greek word *stoicheia* that is translated in 4:3 and 4:9 as "elementary principles" can have a variety of meanings. The idea behind the word is of a first or basic thing from which other things follow. It is used to describe the spoken letters of the alphabet, or the natural elements of which the world is made, or the fundamental principles of an art or science. In Colossians 2, Paul uses *stoicheia* to describe the 'elemental spirits' on which pagan philosophy and religion are built. In Galatians 4, Paul seems to be using this word in a double sense to make his point.

The Old Testament law was certainly part of God's plan. It served an important function. But now that Christ has come, its supervisory role has ended. It no longer is in power over God's people. We are no longer children in slavery. Now we are heirs.

» Implications

(Choose one or more of the following to think about further or to discuss in your group.)

- Why are the trappings of religion so attractive to people? What is it about law-keeping that appeals?

- In what ways are Christians today tempted to go back to slavery regarding:
  - keeping the Old Testament law?

  - keeping other religious rules and laws?

- If Christians are no longer under the law, what role does the Old Testament have for Christians? Look up:
  - Romans 1:1-2

  - Romans 4:23-24

- Romans 15:4

- 1 Corinthians 9:9-10

- 1 Corinthians 10:1-13

- 2 Corinthians 6:16-7:1

- Galatians 3:6-9

- 2 Timothy 3:16-17

- "The proclamation of the gospel is the death knell for all religion." Do you agree with this statement? Why/why not?

» Give thanks and pray

- Give thanks that in Christ there is neither Jew nor Greek, neither slave nor free, neither male nor female, but all are one in Christ Jesus.
- Pray that you would fully understand what it is to be a son or daughter of God, and not fall back into slavery.

STUDY 6

CHRISTIANS: SLAVES OR FREE?

[GALATIANS 4:12-5:12]

1. List some of the restrictions on freedom that are most resented in today's societies.

Paul and the Galatians

Much of the letter to the Galatians hinges on the relationship between Paul, the Galatians and the 'troublers'. Chapter 4 of Galatians starts to spell this out with some personal anecdotes.

We read that on his initial visit, the Galatians warmly received Paul (4:14). We don't know the details of the illness from which Paul suffered (4:13), or why it led him to preach the gospel there. But, presumably (4:14a) it was something unpleasant for them to deal with—we can only speculate.

The Galatians built up a good friendship with the apostle, treating him with great respect (4:14b). But now, Paul is worried, the Galatians have been stirred up to be 'anti-Paul' (4:16-17).

Think back over chapters 1-3.

2. After Paul's departure, what kind of 'trouble' came to the Galatians?

3. How did the Galatian Christians respond to these 'troublers'?

4. Why has Paul written this letter?

Read Galatians 4:12-20.

5. In this passage how does Paul describe his relationship with the Galatians (vv. 19-20)?

Paul's plea

PAUL TAKES SUCH A STRONG STANCE here because the issue at stake is the truth. He is concerned for the truth of the gospel of God's free grace. These 'troublers' are not just disturbing a cosy club—they are theologically false and therefore intolerable.

Paul had seen a group of 'slaves' freed, and now these troublers were persuading them back into slavery.

In adopting a life of law-keeping, the Galatians were giving up the freedom that they had found in the gospel of grace. They were giving up their relationship with God—which is true freedom. Paul can't believe it's happening.

Read Galatians 4:21-5:12.

6. What concerns Paul in 5:1-2?

7. How does the story of Hagar and Sarah help to explain the difference between the Old Covenant and the New Covenant?

8. Why might this have been an especially useful way for Paul to argue his case to the Galatians (4:21)?

Abraham's sons

GOD PROMISED ABRAHAM THAT HE would heal Sarah's infertility, and give them a son of their own, despite their old age. Impatient for a child, Sarah gave her husband a slave girl, Hagar, to breed from. And Hagar gave birth to Ishmael. However, God still fulfilled his promise and, in due time, Isaac was born to Sarah.

This story is used by Paul figuratively to represent slavery under law-keeping versus freedom under the gospel.

Ishmael—although temporarily a son and heir—was always a slave, and the son of a slave. His story stands for Mount Sinai, says Paul (4:24)—that is to say, for the law. Slavery is the symbol of the law. Notice the present position of Israel as far as Paul is concerned. The Jews of today (and that includes the State of Israel) are in slavery. They are just like Ishmael, because, as we saw in study 5, although they are physically the sons of Abraham, they are not true sons of Abraham. They are not the heirs.

Isaac—born of a free woman—is the fulfilment of a promise from God. His story stands for the new covenant—the gospel of the free grace of God in Jesus Christ. Our Jerusalem does not stand on a rocky slope in the state of Israel: our home is the heavenly Jerusalem. And we, like Isaac, are the children of promise—children of supernatural birth:

> But to all who did receive him, who believed in his name, he gave the right to become children of God, who were born, not of blood nor of the will of the flesh nor of the will of man, but of God. (John 1:12-13)

» Implications

(Choose one or more of the following to think about further or to discuss in your group.)

- According to the argument of 4:21-31, who is persecuting whom?

- In what ways are the "children of promise" still persecuted today?

- In 5:2-6 Paul is saying (in effect) that choosing circumcision means asking God to judge you by his perfect law. Where would that put us in relation to Christ?

- If faith is all that counts, does that make the Christian life a matter of passively waiting?

- What possible 'yokes of slavery' can you see that might endanger your spiritual freedom? Are there specific steps you can take to avoid this danger?

- Could you be in danger of imposing a "yoke of slavery" on other Christians (5:10b)? Are there specific steps you can take to avoid this danger?

» Give thanks and pray

- Give thanks that it is for freedom that Christ has set us free.
- Pray for the understanding that in Christ, neither circumcision nor uncircumcision would count for anything, but only faith working through love.
- What else does this passage prompt you to give thanks and pray for?

» STUDY 7
UNNATURAL ACTS
[GALATIANS 5:13-26]

1. What kind of behaviour are most people likely to excuse by saying, "Ah well, it's only natural"?

Called to be free

IN GALATIANS, GOD HAS TAUGHT US so far that we have been freed from the burden of law-keeping.

That is what we have been freed *from*—but what have we been freed *for*? Paul started to spell out the answer in verse 6: "faith working through love".

In verse 13, Paul says we are to "through love serve one another". This, we are taught, is a summary of the entire law (v. 14).

So, is this where the whole argument in Galatians has led us—back to the law?

Read Matthew 7:12, 22:34-40; Romans 13:9-10.

2. Explain how the whole law can be summarized by the command to "love your neighbour as yourself".

Law versus love

WE ARE NOT FREED FROM THE LAW in order to freely sin: we are freed from the law in order to love.

But when you love, you wind up obeying the law! The law and love are, in their content, much the same (v. 14). If I am serving you in love then I won't tell you a lie, or steal from you, or gossip about you.

Well, if that's the case, then what's the difference between the two? There is a double difference: a difference in motive, and a difference in relationship.

Motive

Motivation, or intention, is part of every action. Picture this scene:

> A pretty girl drops an armful of books in front of a library. Three young men rush to pick them up for her: the first because he is a genuine humanitarian who just wants to help; the second because he has been looking at this girl with longing for months and this is his excuse to get an introduction; and the third because he is failing his course and she is top of the class—and this is his chance to plead for a little free coaching.

What they *do* is identical, but they have three different intentions (or motivations).

Relationship

Relationship—our standing or status with others—can also give meaning to our actions. Picture this scene:

> Two athletes sprint as hard as they can around the cinder track of the sports oval. One is running hard because he has been selected for the competition team—and he is motivated by his selection to perform at his best. The other is hoping to win team selection. The first is running with a full heart, eager to please the selectors who have chosen him. The second is trying to force the selectors to make a late, additional selection (namely himself), even though it is against the rules.

The difference in relationship colours their actions.

Act naturally?

The English Standard Version (ESV) of the Bible, which we follow in this Interactive Bible Study, uses the expression 'the flesh' (you'll find it in verses 13, 16, 17, 19 and 24).

However, the Bible's concept of 'flesh' differs from the way we would commonly use the word today. For the Bible, 'flesh' has to do with living in this fallen, sinful world: 'flesh' stands for what we are by nature. So, the same word can also be helpfully translated as the 'sinful nature'.

We can see this meaning illustrated in the lists in verses 19-23 where the sinful nature (the flesh) is contrasted with living by the Spirit.

Read Galatians 5:19-23.

3. Can you think of a short phrase that summarizes the list of acts of the sinful nature?

4. Can you think of a short phrase that summarizes the fruit of the Spirit?

The constant conflict

"But I say," writes Paul, "walk by the Spirit, and you will not gratify the desires of the flesh" (v. 16). Then Paul goes on to describe living naturally (vv. 19-21).

There is a constant conflict between our old nature (the desires and urges that are part of our corrupt human nature), and the Spirit now living in us (v. 17). The conflict continues for as long as we are in our fleshly bodies.

The only way to get out of the conflict is to get out of our sinful nature. And the only way for that to happen is for Jesus to return, or for us to die. As long as we are here, we will be fighting this battle.

The fight is not 'out there'—it is within each one of us. Have you felt the urge to be selfishly ambitious? To compete? To be envious? To be jealous? That is living naturally.

Have you ever become caught up in a little circle of gossip? A little clique? A little group that includes this one and excludes that one? That is living naturally.

Have you ever lost your temper? Had

a fit of rage? Spread discord? Created dissension? Hated someone? That is living naturally.

Picture this scene, a true scene this time. A large supermarket had a blackout a few years ago. It only lasted three minutes. In that time, many thousands of dollars worth of goods were stolen, from all over the shop.

Given the opportunity, ordinary 'honest' people steal. That is living naturally.

Living unnaturally

We must not live according to our nature, but according to the Spirit (v. 16). That is unnatural for us.

The beauty of this is that it is positive.

The law tends to be negative: don't do this, don't do that. Life in the Spirit, on the other hand, is positive: be loving, joyful, peaceful, patient, kind, good, faithful, gentle and self-controlled. We have not been freed in order to indulge our sinful natures, but to serve one another in love. There will be conflict, and we must turn our backs on the works of the flesh.

But positively, there is the fruit of the Spirit. The word 'fruit' is singular—it means 'a crop', not different 'fruits'. There are not meant to be 'kindness' Christians and 'goodness' Christians and 'faithfulness' Christians. Rather, the Christian is meant to be producing a crop of all these things.

We are not passive in this process. We are to "walk by the Spirit" (v. 25). As we fight the inner conflict, as we turn our backs on the flesh, as we pray and work at the crop of the Spirit, God works in us to produce love, joy, peace, patience, kindness, goodness, gentleness, faithfulness and self-control.

Read Galatians 5:13-26.

5. What happens when people live by the sinful nature and not by the Spirit (v. 15 and v. 21)?

6. What makes it so easy to recognize the "works of the flesh"—of living naturally?

» Implications

(Choose one or more of the following to think about further or to discuss in your group.)

- Complete the following table, describing (a) the relationship, or standing, before God; and (b) the motivation, or intention, of the law-keeper versus the Christian (the man or woman of the Spirit).

	Law-keeper	Christian
Relationship with God		
Motive for action		

- Do 'sins of the flesh' only turn up in R-rated movies? What 'sins of the flesh' might you find in a G-rated movie?

- If Paul had lost his temper, would he have thought that an unnatural thing to do?

- Why are ambition, factions and jealousy "works of the flesh"? What impact might they have on the lives of others?

- Should Christians expect to be able to conquer the sin in their lives?

- Looking at the list of the fruit of the Spirit, which two of those qualities are you best at? Which two do you need to work hardest at?

- What steps can you take this week to cooperate more with God in growing the crop of the Spirit in your life?

» Give thanks and pray

- Give thanks that because of the victory of Jesus, you have been redeemed from the sinful nature.
- Pray that the Spirit would increase his fruit in you, and enable you to walk by the Spirit.

» STUDY 8

TWO WAYS TO LIVE

[GALATIANS 6]

1. How do you think most people would react to the hard line that Galatians draws between grace and law—between the genuine and the false way to be right with God?

In Galatians, God is teaching us to draw the line: you either trust Jesus or you trust yourself. There are only two ways to live.

Is this all remote and 'other worldly'? Or does it say something about how we live our daily lives here and now?

In chapter 6, Galatians applies this 'two ways' thinking to our method of daily living—our method of relating to each other. And it does this by looking at three specific applications: restoration, repayment, and reaping.

In each of these, it is contrasting two people—the legalist (the law-keeper) and the Christian (the Spirit-led person).

Restoration

Read Galatians 6:1-5.

2. In what manner should you deal with a brother caught in any transgression (or sin)?

3. What is the danger in doing this?

4. What should be your motivation in dealing with a brother caught in sin?

5. Does your brother's sin show your own spiritual superiority? What should it show you?

» Implications

(Choose one or more of the following to think about further or to discuss in your group.)

- Does Paul contradict himself in verses 2 and 5? How can you fit these two ideas together?

- How would you feel if you were "caught in any transgression" (v. 1) by a Christian brother or sister? How would you want that brother or sister to treat you?

- Picture this: you have discovered that a Christian friend of yours has fallen into the sin of adultery—what steps will you take to "restore him [or her] in a spirit of gentleness" (v. 1)?

- What excuses might they make for their behaviour? How would you respond to those excuses?

- What (if anything) will you say to other Christians?

- How would a legalist (i.e. law-keeper) deal with someone who falls into sin?

Repayment

Read Galatians 6:6.

6. What does it mean to "share all good things" with your instructor (in the word of God)?

7. Is this optional?

8. Does this necessarily apply only to money?

» Implications

- List three ways in which you might be able to "share all good things" with your teacher of God's word. (Be creative!)
  -
  -
  -

- How might a legalist respond to the necessity of sharing all things with his or her instructor?

Reaping

Read Galatians 6:7-10.

9. Who controls this sowing and reaping process (v. 7)?

10. Some "sow" (that is, invest their time, mind and energy) to please the sinful nature. What will they reap?

11. What will the one who sows to please the Spirit reap?

12. Does the reaping happen very soon after the sowing?

13. Why do we reap what we sow?

14. When should we do good (v. 10)?

15. To whom should we do good?

16. To whom should we give priority?

» Implications

(Choose one or more of the following to think about further or to discuss in your group.)

- List some things in which you *should not* invest your time, energy or thinking.

- List some things in which you *should* invest your time, energy or thinking.

- We all have limited financial resources, and much of the world is crying out in poverty and hunger for our help. Given the unlimited needs of the world, what priorities should you have in generously sharing your money? (Consult Galatians 6:6, 6:10 and 1 Timothy 5:8.)

Parting words

As Paul closes his letter to the Galatians, he aims a few parting shots at those who are trying to compel the Galatians to submit to law. In doing so, he highlights the contrast there is between the gospel of grace and law-keeping, between the freedom of the Spirit and the slavery of legalism. His final words are worth thinking over as a fitting conclusion to all that Galatians has been saying.

Read Galatians 6:11-18.

17. Who are these legalists trying to impress?

18. What are these legalists trying to avoid?

19. What matters to Paul?

20. What doesn't matter to Paul?

21. How do these verses summarize the concerns of the whole letter?

22. Sum up what you have learned from your study of Galatians.

» Give thanks and pray

- Give thanks for those who have taught the word to you.
- Pray that you, like Paul, would boast in nothing but the cross of our Lord Jesus Christ.
- What else does this passage, and the rest of the letter to the Galatians, prompt you to give thanks and pray for?

Feedback on this resource

We really appreciate getting feedback about our resources—not just suggestions for how to improve them, but also positive feedback and ways they can be used. We especially love to hear that the resources may have helped someone in their Christian growth.

You can send feedback to us via the 'Feedback' menu in our online store, or write to us at PO Box 225, Kingsford NSW 2032, Australia.

Matthias Media is an evangelical publishing ministry that seeks to persuade all Christians of the truth of God's purposes in Jesus Christ as revealed in the Bible, and equip them with high-quality resources, so that by the work of the Holy Spirit they will:

- abandon their lives to the honour and service of Christ in daily holiness and decision-making
- pray constantly in Christ's name for the fruitfulness and growth of his gospel
- speak the Bible's life-changing word whenever and however they can— in the home, in the world and in the fellowship of his people.

It was in 1988 that we first started pursuing this mission, and in God's kindness we now have more than 300 different ministry resources being used all over the world. These resources range from Bible studies and books through to training courses and audio sermons.

To find out more about our large range of very useful resources, and to access samples and free downloads, visit our website:

www.matthiasmedia.com.au

How to buy our resources

1. Direct from us over the internet:
   - in the US: www.matthiasmedia.com
   - in Australia and the rest of the world: www.matthiasmedia.com.au

2. Direct from us by phone:
   - in the US: 1 866 407 4530
   - in Australia: 1800 814 360 (Sydney: 9663 1478)
   - international: +61-2-9663-1478

> Register at our website for our **free** regular email update to receive information about the latest new resources, **exclusive special offers**, and free articles to help you grow in your Christian life and ministry.

3. Through a range of outlets in various parts of the world. Visit **www.matthiasmedia.com.au/information/contact-us** for details about recommended retailers in your part of the world, including www.thegoodbook.co.uk in the United Kingdom.

4. Trade enquiries can be addressed to:
   - in the US and Canada: sales@matthiasmedia.com
   - in Australia and the rest of the world: sales@matthiasmedia.com.au

Other Interactive and Topical Bible Studies from Matthias Media

Our Interactive Bible Studies (IBS) and Topical Bible Studies (TBS) are a valuable resource to help you keep feeding from God's word. The IBS series works through passages and books of the Bible; the TBS series pulls together the Bible's teaching on topics such as money or prayer. As at May 2010, the series contains the following titles:

Beyond Eden
GENESIS 1-11
Authors: Phillip Jensen and Tony Payne, 9 studies

Out of Darkness
EXODUS 1-18
Author: Andrew Reid, 8 studies

The Shadow of Glory
EXODUS 19-40
Author: Andrew Reid, 7 studies

The One and Only
DEUTERONOMY
Author: Bryson Smith, 8 studies

The Good, the Bad and the Ugly
JUDGES
Author: Mark Baddeley, 10 studies

Famine and Fortune
RUTH
Authors: Barry Webb and David Höhne, 4 studies

Renovator's Dream
NEHEMIAH
Authors: Phil Campbell and Greg Clarke, 7 studies

The Eye of the Storm
JOB
Author: Bryson Smith, 6 studies

The Search for Meaning
ECCLESIASTES
Author: Tim McMahon, 9 studies

Two Cities
ISAIAH
Authors: Andrew Reid and Karen Morris, 9 studies

Kingdom of Dreams
DANIEL
Authors: Andrew Reid and Karen Morris, 9 studies

Burning Desire
OBADIAH AND MALACHI
Authors: Phillip Jensen and Richard Pulley, 6 studies

Warning Signs
JONAH
Author: Andrew Reid, 6 studies

On That Day
ZECHARIAH
Author: Tim McMahon, 8 studies

Full of Promise
THE BIG PICTURE OF THE O.T.
Authors: Phil Campbell and Bryson Smith, 8 studies

The Good Living Guide
MATTHEW 5:1-12
Authors: Phillip Jensen and Tony Payne, 9 studies

News of the Hour
MARK
Authors: Peter Bolt and Tony Payne, 10 studies

Proclaiming the Risen Lord
LUKE 24-ACTS 2
Author: Peter Bolt, 6 studies

Mission Unstoppable
ACTS
Author: Bryson Smith, 10 studies

The Free Gift of Life
ROMANS 1-5
Author: Gordon Cheng, 8 studies

The Free Gift of Sonship
ROMANS 6-11
Author: Gordon Cheng, 8 studies

The Freedom of Christian Living
ROMANS 12-16
Author: Gordon Cheng, 7 studies

Free for All
GALATIANS
Authors: Phillip Jensen and Kel Richards, 8 studies

Walk this Way
EPHESIANS
Author: Bryson Smith, 8 studies

Partners for Life
PHILIPPIANS
Author: Tim Thorburn, 8 studies

The Complete Christian
COLOSSIANS
Authors: Phillip Jensen and Tony Payne, 8 studies

To the Householder
1 TIMOTHY
Authors: Phillip Jensen and Greg Clarke, 9 studies

Run the Race
2 TIMOTHY
Author: Bryson Smith, 6 studies

The Path to Godliness
TITUS
Authors: Phillip Jensen and Tony Payne, 7 studies

From Shadow to Reality
HEBREWS
Author: Joshua Ng, 10 studies

The Implanted Word
JAMES
Authors: Phillip Jensen and Kirsten Birkett, 8 studies

Homeward Bound
1 PETER
Authors: Phillip Jensen and Tony Payne, 10 studies

All You Need to Know
2 PETER
Author: Bryson Smith, 6 studies

The Vision Statement
REVELATION
Author: Greg Clarke, 9 studies

Bold I Approach
PRAYER
Author: Tony Payne, 6 studies

Cash Values
MONEY
Author: Tony Payne, 5 studies

Sing for Joy
SINGING IN CHURCH
Author: Nathan Lovell, 6 studies

The Blueprint
DOCTRINE
Authors: Phillip Jensen and Tony Payne, 9 studies

Woman of God
THE BIBLE ON WOMEN
Author: Terry Blowes, 8 studies

Also from Matthias Media

Galatians on MP3 CD

If you would like further input on Galatians, you'll find this set of eight talks very helpful. Phillip Jensen expounds the passages looked at in *Free for All*, providing additional insights and ideas, and tying the material together in a way that is possible in a sermon but not in a group Bible study. The talks are an ideal accompaniment to the studies, especially for group leaders who want to do some additional preparation.

1. Damned angels and gospel perverters (Galatians 1:1-10)
2. Was Paul authentic? (Galatians 1-2)
3. Faith + anything = nothing (Galatians 2:11-21)
4. The cursed Jesus (Galatians 3:1-18)
5. Who are Abraham's heirs? (Galatians 3:19-4:11)
6. Christians: slaves or free? (Galatians 4:12-5:12)
7. Christians: natural or unnatural? (Galatians 5:13-26)
8. Christians: caring or indifferent? (Galatians 6)

FOR MORE INFORMATION OR TO ORDER CONTACT:

Matthias Media
Telephone: +61-2-9663-1478
Facsimile: +61-2-9663-3265
Email: sales@matthiasmedia.com.au
www.matthiasmedia.com.au

Matthias Media (USA)
Telephone: 1-866-407-4530
Facsimile: 724-964-8166
Email: sales@matthiasmedia.com
www.matthiasmedia.com

Also from Matthias Media

Pathway Bible Guides

Pathway Bible Guides are simple, straightforward, easy-to-read Bible studies, ideal for groups who are new to studying the Bible, or groups with limited time for study.

We've designed the studies to be short and easy to use, with an uncomplicated vocabulary. At the same time, we've tried to do justice to the passages being studied, and to model good Bible-reading principles. Pathway Bible Guides are simple without being simplistic; no-nonsense without being no-content.

As at May 2010, the series contains the following titles:

- Beginning with God (Genesis 1-12)
- Getting to Know God (Exodus 1-20)
- The Art of Living (Proverbs)
- Seeing Things God's Way (Daniel)
- Fear and Freedom (Matthew 8-12)
- Following Jesus (Luke 9-12)
- Peace with God (Romans)
- Church Matters (1 Corinthians 1-7)
- Standing Firm (1 Thessalonians)

For more information or to order contact:

Matthias Media
Telephone: +61-2-9663-1478
Facsimile: +61-2-9663-3265
Email: sales@matthiasmedia.com.au
www.matthiasmedia.com.au

Matthias Media (USA)
Telephone: 1-866-407-4530
Facsimile: 724-964-8166
Email: sales@matthiasmedia.com
www.matthiasmedia.com

Also from Matthias Media

The God Who Saves
5 Bible studies for people who think that faith matters

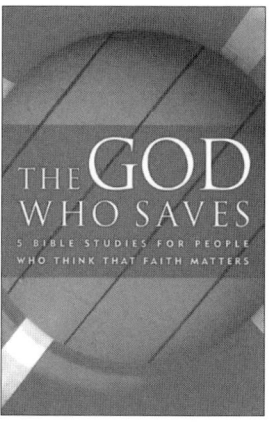

Can we be sure that we will be saved? Is there anything special we need to do to be saved? Is going to church or being religious enough to get us over the line?

Join Mark Gilbert as he looks at what the Bible tells us about true salvation. Learn about how God saves us, why God saves us and what we are saved from.

Perhaps you know someone who, because of their background or upbringing, believes that being religious is the key to their salvation. Perhaps they haven't fully grasped their freedom in Christ. These studies are ideal for such a situation, and can be done either in a group setting or a one-to-one context.

Leader's notes are available as a free download:
http://www.matthiasmedia.com.au/tgws/

FOR MORE INFORMATION OR TO ORDER CONTACT:

Matthias Media
Telephone: +61-2-9663-1478
Facsimile: +61-2-9663-3265
Email: sales@matthiasmedia.com.au
www.matthiasmedia.com.au

Matthias Media (USA)
Telephone: 1-866-407-4530
Facsimile: 724-964-8166
Email: sales@matthiasmedia.com
www.matthiasmedia.com